Robots at Home

Christine Zuchora-Walske

Lerner Publications Company
Minneapolis

Lerner Publications Company
A division of Lerner Publishing Group, Inc.
241 First Avenue North
Minneapolis, MN 55401 USA

Cover photo: Aibo was created by Sony. He is the first-ever home robot made for entertainment and can express emotions like a real dog.

For reading levels and more information, look up this title at www.lernerbooks.com.

Library of Congress Cataloging-in-Publication Data

Zuchora-Walske, Christine, author.
    Robots at home / by Christine Zuchora-Walske.
       pages   cm. — (Lightning bolt books™—Robots everywhere!)
    Includes index.
    ISBN 978-1-4677-4054-8 (lib. bdg. : alk. paper)
    ISBN 978-1-4677-4691-5 (eBook)
    1. Robots—Juvenile literature. I. Title.
    TJ211.2.Z83 2015
    629.8'92—dc23   2013041562

Manufactured in the United States of America
1 – BP – 7/15/14

Table of Contents

What is a Robot?

A robot is a machine. It has sensors and can move. It is built to do work for people.

This robot is named Asimo.

These robots build cars. They can work without taking breaks.

People use robots for hard or boring work. Robots do many different jobs. But all robots have much in common.

A robot must sense the world around it. It uses sensors to do this. Robots sense light, sound, or touch.

A robot named Tomorrow can play volleyball. It has cameras to sense where the ball is.

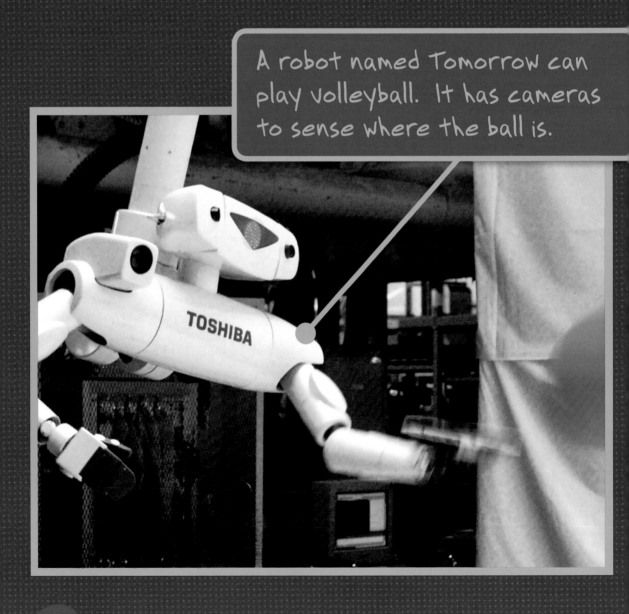

A robot must be able to move. It needs energy to do this. Robots use gas, batteries, or sunlight for energy.

Many robots use wheels to move around.

Scientists write computer programs that control robots.

A robot uses a computer to think. Scientists fill the computer with instructions. These instructions are called a program. The program controls the robot.

Lots of people have home robots. These robots help in many ways. Some do chores. Others keep people company. Some even help people have fun!

Some robots wash floors. Using a robot is much easier than using a mop.

Housework Robots

Some robots do chores people don't like doing.

This robot cleans the floor while its owner relaxes.

One kind of robot vacuums floors. Its sensors can find dirt. The robot spends more time on these spots.

Another robot cleans roof gutters. It scrapes away leaves with brushes. Robots can also clean pools. They sink to the bottom. Then they scrub the floor and sides.

A robot can mow lawns. Its sensors find the edges. It stays inside them. The mower robot also senses objects. It sees trees and pets. It mows around them.

This robot lawn mower is powered by the sun. It has solar panels to collect electricity.

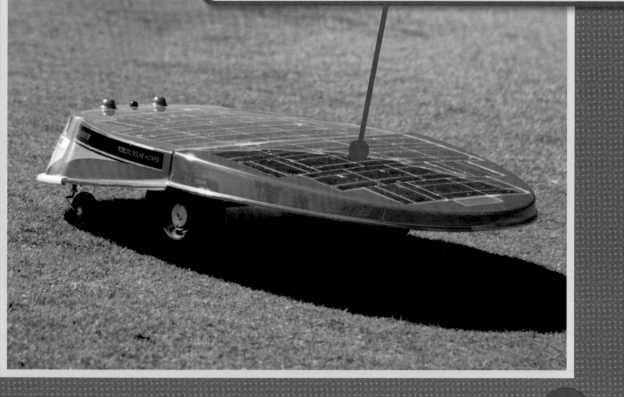

Nobody likes cleaning up cat litter. But robotic litter boxes make it easy. Sensors see when a cat has left the box. Then the box cleans itself.

Scientists are working on butler robots. These robots will search for lost items. They will use cameras and other sensors. Then the robots will put the items away.

This butler robot is named HERB. The name stands for Home Exploring Robot Butler.

Personal Robots

Personal robots help people with daily tasks.

Scientists are working on robot cars to drive people around. Sensors on the roof watch where the car is going.

A robotic alarm clock can help you wake up. It jumps off your nightstand. It rolls around the floor. It makes noise. You must get out of bed to turn it off.

An alarm clock called Clocky hides in a new place each day.

A robot named Autom tells its owner to exercise and eat right.

Some robots help people eat well. One type of robot sits on the kitchen counter. It moves its head to follow you around. It asks about what you eat. It gives advice on healthful food choices.

Therapy robots are sort of like pets. They keep people company. They help people feel more calm.

This therapy robot is named Paro. It looks like a baby seal.

ぼくの名前は
タマ ちゃん
男の子です

Robot wheelchairs can help older people. They have arms that grab objects. They have wheels to carry people around. The wheelchairs let older adults live on their own.

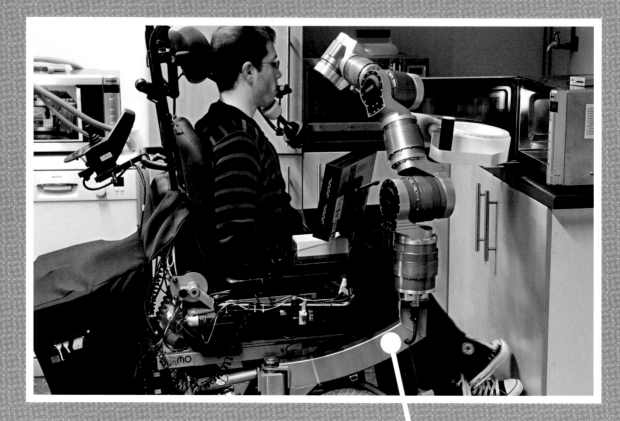

A robot scientist tests a robot wheelchair's arms at a university in Germany.

Scientists are working on new robots to help people with disabilities. These robots will open doors. They will hold objects. They will even cook food.

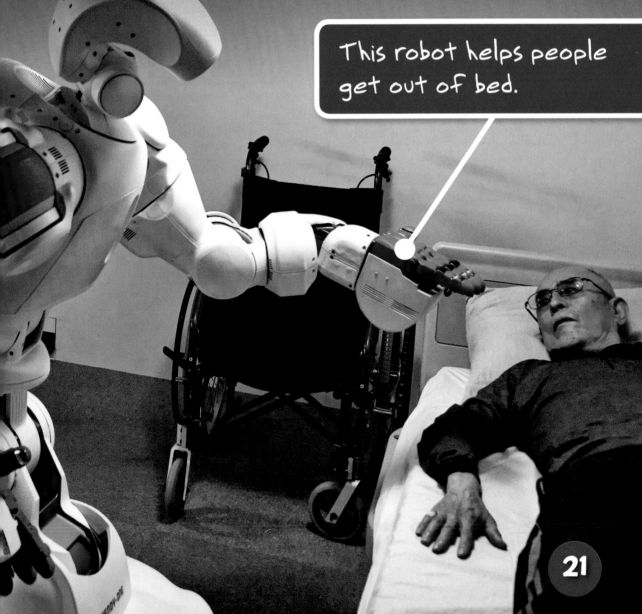

This robot helps people get out of bed.

Toy Robots

Toy robots help kids learn how to solve problems. Kids design and build robots. Then they program and run the robots.

Designing toy robots gives kids skills they can use to become robot scientists.

Toy robots help with more than just learning. They are also fun to use!

Some toy robots look like animals, including dinosaurs.

Robot kits help kids learn about robots. Kids can build robots and create programs. They use the robots to play games. The robots can crawl, kick, and throw. Some schools even have robot-building contests.

These robots were built by kids for a competition in Malaysia. Competitors came from all around the world.

Kids create their own programs for this robot.

One toy robot looks like a robot vacuum. But it does much more than clean floors. Kids create their own programs for it. They control its sensors and movement.

This rolling robot is named Sphero. It can also change colors.

One kind of robot ball has a sense of balance. You can program it to roll around. It can even measure the space where it moves.

Kids can program small, human-shaped robots. The robots remember faces and voices. They can walk and talk.

Several colleges worked together to create a walking robot named DARwin.

Robot Scientists

- A robot scientist is called a roboticist. People who become roboticists go to college for at least four years.

- Robots combine science, math, computer programming, and design. Robot scientists study all those subjects.

- Robot scientists may spend the day reading diagrams, programming robots, and testing new sensors. They also talk with people who will use the robots.

- People who build home robots think about making the robots easy to use and fix. They find ways to keep the robots from wearing out.

Fun Facts

- Leonardo da Vinci drew up plans for a robot in 1495. It looked like a human and had armor. As far as we know, he never built it.

- One home robot can identify different foods and drinks. It moves its head, and its mouth lights up when it talks. But it once mistook a person's hand for a piece of ham!

- All together, robot vacuums have sucked up more than 2 billion pounds (900,000 kilograms) of dirt.

- A Czech playwright invented the word *robot* in 1920. It comes from a word that means "slave."

- In some Middle Eastern nations, robot jockeys race on camels.

Glossary

butler: a household servant

disability: an injury or illness that makes daily life harder

program: a set of computer instructions

robot: a machine that does work for humans. A robot must be able to move and sense the world around it.

robotic: something that uses a robot to carry out tasks

sensor: a part of a robot that lets it understand its environment

therapy: treatment designed to heal someone

Further Reading

Ceceri, Kathy. *Robotics: Discover the Science and Technology of the Future with 20 Projects.* White River Junction, VT: Nomad Press, 2012.

Domaine, Helena. *Robotics.* Minneapolis: Lerner Publications, 2006.

Galileo Educational Network: Robotics
http://www.galileo.org/robotics

Idaho Public Television Dialogue for Kids: Robots
http://idahoptv.org/dialogue4kids/season10/robots

NASA Robots Storybook
http://www.nasa.gov/audience/forstudents/k-4/stories/ames-robot-storybook-text.html

Stewart, Melissa. *Robots.* Washington, DC: National Geographic Children's Books, 2014.

Tech Museum: Robotics
http://www.thetech.org/exhibits/online/robotics

Index

Photo Acknowledgments

The images in this book are used with the permission of: © Dikiiy/Shutterstock Images, pp. 2, 5, 23; © catwalker/Shutterstock Images, pp. 4, 30; © Koji Sasahara/AP Images, p. 6; © Darq/Shutterstock Images, p. 7; © Andrey Novikov/Shutterstock Images, p. 8; © nui7711/Shutterstock Images, p. 9; © Jirsak/Shutterstock Images, p. 10; © Oleksiy Maksymenko/All Canada Photos/SuperStock, pp. 11, 28; © Paul Sakuma/AP Images, p. 12; © Universal Images Group/SuperStock, p. 13; © Mark Duncan/AP Images, p. 14; © Tony Avelar/Bloomberg/Getty Images, p. 15; © Steve Jurvetson/Flickr, p. 16; © Artur Tarwacki, p. 17; © Zhang Jun/Xinhua Press/Corbis, p. 18; © Haruyoshi Yamaguchi/Corbis, p. 19; © A2942/_Ingo Wagner/dpa/Corbis, p. 20; © Randy Olson/National Geographic/SuperStock, p. 21; © CHEN WS/Shutterstock Images, pp. 22, 24, 31; © jeremiah/Flickr, p. 25; © Lachlan Hardy/Flickr, p. 26; © Arne Kuilman/Flickr, p. 27.

Front cover: © Hulton Archive/Getty Images.